Creative Writing
Anthology **2010**

Poetry

egg box

UEA Creative Writing Anthology 2010

Poetry

First published by Egg Box Publishing, 2010

International © retained by individual authors

This book is sold subject to the condition that it shall not, by way of trade or otherwise, be lent, resold, hired out, stored in a retrieval system, or otherwise circulated without the publisher's prior consent in any form of binding or cover other than that in which it is published and without a similar condition including this condition being imposed on the subsequent purchaser.

A CIP record for this book is available from the British Library.

UEA Creative Writing Anthology 2010 is typeset in Oranda 11pt on 12.5pt Leading.

Printed and bound by:
Printed in Great Britain by the MPG Books Group,
Bodmin and King's Lynn

Designed and typeset by:
Kettle of Fish Design, Norwich
www.kettleoffishdesign.com

Proofed by:
Sarah Gooderson

Distributed by:
Central Books

ISBN:
978-0955939969

Acknowledgements

UEA Creative Writing Anthology 2010

Thanks to the following for making this anthology possible: the Malcolm Bradbury Memorial Fund, the Centre for Creative and Performing Arts at the University of East Anglia and The School of Literature & Creative Writing at UEA in partnership with Egg Box Publishing.

We'd also like to thank the following people:

Trezza Azzopardi, Jean Boase-Beier, Amit Chaudhuri, Jon Cook, Andrew Cowan, Giles Foden, Sarah Gooderson, Lavinia Greenlaw, Rachel Hore, Kathryn Hughes, Michael Lengsfield, Jean McNeil, Natalie Mitchell, Rob Ritchie, Michèle Roberts, George Szirtes and Val Taylor.

Nathan Hamilton at Egg Box Publishing, and Catrin & Dylan Lloyd-Edwards at Kettle of Fish Design.

Editorial team:
Whitney Austin
Tom Benn
Carrie Chandler
Georgie Codd
Catherine Etoe
Tim Harding
Annabel Howard
Alex Ivey
Julia Webb

UEA Creative Writing Anthology 2010

Contents

Foreword
Lavinia Greenlaw and George Szirtes i

Poetry
....8

Contributors
Theodore Best 10
Claire-Jane Carter 17
Prue Chamberlayne 23
Tim Cockburn 31
Bryan Heiser 38
Mary Laxton 43
David Lebor 49
Katherine Venn 57
Julia Webb 64
Sam Wright 71

Foreword

by **Lavinia Greenlaw** and **George Szirtes**

Poetry is concentration of language, the cry becoming song and speech at once. There is no single route to that becoming: cry can become poetry in many ways. This variety is the very life of poetry. The new builds on the old in its own organic way, picking up what it needs and can comprehend – and it comprehends by listening intently to all that passes and to its own desire, even – perhaps particularly – in the formation of the poem.

For that reason there has never been a house style at UEA, there is only the offer of intense listening to the poem on its own terms, trying to understand the soil from which it rises, noting the landscape around it, then encouraging the formation of the cry into song and speech. That is the process the contributors to this anthology are involved in: it is what makes them different and differently valuable.

Theodore Best's poems begin from nature and passion but deploy elemental forces with ever more wit and precision becoming increasingly inventive. Under the invention lies a fidelity to the terms of ballad and song. People and creatures are observed but are yearning to become parts of a continuing energy, a kind of fire.

Prue Chamberlayne shows how ekphrasis, art that is a response to a work of art, can activate a poet's imagination. Her chosen subjects act as a lens through which she focuses her intensely visceral and precise exploration of the elemental and physical. Landscape too is opened up to its machinery and depths.

Tim Cockburn works with an extraordinarily sharp ear, educated by his reading. The poems may seem light, almost incidental at times, but they are like remarks dropped in a marbled hall, balancing the weight of the hall with a kind of off-hand classicism, the effect being far from flip, but graceful, acute and strangely grave.

Claire-Jane Carter has a gift for perceptual mobility. Her poems are as focused as they are unanchored, allowing the kind of disorientation that makes us unusually conscious and sensitised. Her deep consideration of her subject ensures that her poems capture the essence of our extreme and fundamental experience of the world.

The gravity of Bryan Heiser's poems rests on very firm foundations. They rise through form and through dramatisation of experience, drawing on the resources of literary tradition to present the reader with a renewed pathos and a new keenness of desire. History and the memory are united through ardour, grace and myth.

There is a constant tussle between intellectual and emotional energy in Mary Laxton's poems. Ideas are bursting to enter the field of fully-felt experience, because somehow the two must belong to the same world. They jostle and press against the surface of the language, are vibrant and troubled. Something very important is at stake here.

David Lebor's poems are drawn from the tension that holds things both apart and in place. They operate out of oscillation and resonance, and draw us into the cracks and corners of vision and emotion. This fragmentation extends to his phrasing, which breaks open or breaks down and yet resolves into poems of great sensitivity and depth.

Katherine Venn makes dextrous use of form to amplify unspoken tensions – between child and parent, the world and the self, or those continuous internal adjustments and complications through which we process experience. Her calm intelligence realises this in poems that are delightfully exacting and clear.

Julia Webb employs the surreal to articulate the extreme and unspoken currents of life: death, violence, secrets, desire. In her work, language and image refract under the pressure of their subject. She leads us into uncomfortable and exciting territory with remarkable imaginative force.

Like delicate instruments, Sam Wright's poems depend on tiny perfected movements. In some ways anecdotal, in other ways like tentative philosophical statements on the enigmatic and paradoxical puzzles of perception, they hoist a universe into place and gaze at it with a certain irony, trying to shape and feel its nature.

LG and GS

UEA Creative Writing Anthology 2010

Poetry

Theodore Best
Claire-Jane Carter
Prue Chamberlayne
Tim Cockburn
Bryan Heiser
Mary Laxton
David Lebor
Katherine Venn
Julia Webb
Sam Wright

Theodore Best

Give Me a Red Breast and a Song
Incidentally
English as a Foreign Language
Owl

Give Me a Red Breast and a Song

I have sung down branches
to their sticky booby-traps.
Near things with bald wings
felt serenaded.

I have sung by the roundabout
in the middle of the night.
The lamplight was lamplight.
Nobody told me.

I have sung in gardens at hoses.
I have noted the cold of the flat black grass.
They say I am a territorial beast.

I have eaten from a fat-ball
hanging on a cherry tree.
Through those squares of hard air
what was watching?

I have eaten the beetle
crawling on my lookout.
A green spot's appeared there –
shiny, like a beetle.

I have eaten a white knotted worm.
I have learnt not to turn from the whisker-claw.
They say I am a territorial beast.

Sometimes things look at me
like we belong together.
Show me a red breast
not a soft beak.

Others throw sticks at me
or screech like the whisker-claw.
All this is useable
for a nest in the wind.

I have harried green rubber in flowerbeds.
I have wrestled the edges of silver.
They say I am a territorial beast.

Though I fear the wind stopping
and a death in the dead grass,
breast upward, head downward,
neck awry,

I know only this:
that my voice is as big
as the one bush it's filled.
One song,

and all manner of life sees a nesting place.

Incidentally

sometimes I laugh so hard I spill my coffee
and then the thing is to go on laughing,
my mouth eight bars glinting in candlelight,
while my napkinless hands hover like a pair of bees
transfixed by the flower they can see themselves in.

English as a Foreign Language

today
a man stands in a bottom corner
by an equals sign

his arms
are limp black daffodils
blue dots arc from his eyes

yesterday his mouth was a bowl

*

three clouds rise
from a young man's frown

in the last he's on his knees
and a woman with green cheeks
says of course I will exclamation mark

*

there are eleven dashes on the board

we have

s blank r blank n
d blank p
blank t y

under this
a man with x's for eyes
hangs by his neck from a gallows

some of the alphabet watches

*

a house has a broken window

a woman in the doorway
has one hand on her cheek
and a mouth like a boomerang

at the right of the board
a man with a big bag and a mask
is running

above them

Passive Voice

*

a man is on the phone

his right foot is in the mouth of a dog

at the left of the board
a woman with a dot for a mouth
has answered a call

a squiggly line connects them

*

today
the board is covered in fruit

tomorrow it will be vegetables

next week animals the names of meat
cutlery cook cooker the kitchen

bedroom bathroom

living room on Friday

Owl

The owl dangles in dusk, pounding stillness,
each wing a swishable map of the alveolate air,
each feather-tip the needle of a seismograph.

I stalk this half-aflight gargoyle,
quiet enough to see his liquid eye set
and his body fold like a bag around a rock as he drops
to kill behind a heather-bush.

Moments later,
his wings are ratchets hoisting daggers into mist;
his belly melts the flesh from bone and fur.
My tongue would learn much from a tail
that planes the air to its fulcrum.

Instead, I scuff a gravel-patch
and I'm lit by a face like a Venn-diagram,
the shadow of myself
thrown over the hedge behind me
like an overcoat.

In time, my body hardens
but the owl's near wing has risen.

Over the field he bounds toward his mouths.

Theodore Best grew up in Dorset. Having moved to London to study Psychology and later Philosophy, he worked as an actor and English language teacher. He currently lives in Norwich, where he is on the committee of the UEA Beekeeping Society.

Claire-Jane Carter

Dartmoor, at this time
To Follow
New Year

Dartmoor, at this time

we are half running with heather hair
our feet hares darting over dark peat
as the heathen moon rises and the tors
beat down on the grim moor

thin in the mud and fernsam we hide
skin and bone to the grimestone
rushing through the night in
time to the starlight ahead as
owls howl and fight
under separating constellations

our wandering slows the shields spin
as we seek the old wounds beneath
the round potter's wheel
wet with dewed clay
has ground to a silt halt

and now
as dawn shatters in the wind
horned bushes thaw
and claws fall to the loam

To Follow

Remembering, I wondered if I moved first
or if you touched me
did it seem like I had been waiting

you placed this rock in my hand
and closed my fingertips over it

softly unclothed
where your hollow has grown cold
I wake and wake again
into dark
fingering the creases in the sheets
lost in lines of cloth without maps
or patterned alignment
of tors and stars
to landmark the bed

the streetlamps part with the trees at dawn

the preserves stiffen on the table
and smoked tea brings in the rain
as I make to leave

I have been sent out to follow you

if you see something
anything
reach out, touch wood
mark the moss

bend the bracken aside in places
press your hands into the peat
lie down in the sand
leave footprints well away from the waves

high above wide lands
the path runs
along broken limestone ridges
and descends between clefts
and downy pines

at times I find yarn leading from
still tarns
and cairns built on flat ground

in these days the wind
has been known to file the sky
to thin blade
did you ever watch the lightning crawl
like a broken man across the cliffs

two hundred feet above the waves
I crawl along a black zawn
seabirds scream and spit
they pause mid flight
as if they would choose to fall
I watch silently
as their bodies plummet past
to rip apart with sudden wings in the spray

the light is turning
previously blank rock jostles with minerals in the gold
elements of driftwood, glass and bone converse with the shingle
learning the shape of the sea
until dark

crouched boulders wash their secret parts in salt water

I head inland

a gullet in the ground
has swallowed the way

no fenland glimmering in the mist but
the flint lips of a newly
scoured maw
where the path has caved in

I lean against the hill

unmapped and in tatters
the track in my head unwinds
to its thread ends
they drift
and catch
in dead sea thrift

will you let yourself be lost

my hands are hatched
with such regular notches
I can count the days spent
following
lines split into the land
my fingers knot bladderwrack in my lap
mottled, brackish knuckles crack
like rotting gulls' eggs

the door stutters on the latch

as the deads' hair grows from bone
lichen beards our walls

so I stay awake

and cycle back and forth through these days
slow without your slipstream

the trees are so simple now
they drift in the road

New Year

The moorhen wails from a central eddy
of a lake
a dark sky and a dark car on the road
flare together
statues of horse, tall streetlamps
and the slant shadows
of fences
fall gradually to the ground
outside a slow
dumbfound town

Again the hail rises out
high across the marsh
and fate cards
stack wide and blank
at the side of paths
so hollow in the throat
the owl flies
to a dark loch
between two people

under these smoking trees
their faces are sweet
and blunt at the edges

Claire-Jane Carter is a climber who, after studying in the flatlands of Norfolk for six years, has moved to Sheffield to be in cycling distance of vertical geology. She has an affinity for all landscapes, contoured or not, and is interested in the mythic, historic and present experiences of our environment.

Prue Chamberlayne

Spider-girl
Anish Kapoor (I)
Anish Kapoor (II)
Anish Kapoor (III)

Dunlins at Dawlish
Ceilhes
December in Aveyron
Maisemore Weir

Spider-girl

(after Louise Bourgeois, Tate Modern)

I know this place inside her rickety legs,
against the cage, my mother's corset.

Beneath her glass ball sac, by threadbare chair
I am her creature, safe from the reach of limbs

that grab my siblings, bang their heads and sting.
I swallow horror, learn to glance past, forget.

Bound to escape ten heads jammed in a bed,
my carapace, and mending webs, I turn to missile;

eyeball to eyeball mirrors draw me in –
spat from volcanic rock.

Anish Kapoor (I)

rhizomes, turds, snails, whelks,
pile up, sink, slip, envelop us,
we're dwarfed
in temples, antheaps, wattle latrines

a giant ovary
a leaning amphora
arches towards the sky
we love it mounting

those wild forces
those pounding hooves
that draw the sun
sly moon forever

pulling strings
we crave these body tiltings
our being
too blunt when willed.

Anish Kapoor (II)

on neat cut rails
the red wax portal shivers
through the towering onion arch
the shaved excess makes spatterings
of beetroot mush

I want the waiting to be over
I know the crack will be a scythe
a blinding light of horror
feels coiled intestines lurch
and vulva twitch and sigh.

Anish Kapoor (III)

a giant yellow sun looks flat
as does the bare breast wall –
side views reveal a lurching, swallowing hollow
and curves I'd love to touch –
a thought allowed of this cool stone.

Dunlins at Dawlish

What seems at first a horde of scurrying mice
turns into Lilliputian ballerinas,
a glissade in black leotards up the beach,
perfect round pebbles, strands of seaweed, ahead
of the encroaching skirt of sea. In flash and twist,
like thoughts too quick to catch, white undersides
turn striped, then black – I'm poised for their departure.
I long to share wing-beating acrobatics,
hang between air and body-being, dissolve
in blue-grey haze, soul-stretched in salt-filled wind.
But they drop back to peck on drier sand,
circle in single flurry to the looped ebb,
the grey brown sheen doubling their ruffled speckles,
heads held high as bar-trained dancers, spindly
legs held taut against the sandy swill.

Ceilhes

From vast bare hilltops,
we drop into dark shade
between tall buildings,
up alleyways slit glimpses
of an old stone church;
cool smell of history tugs,
Ceilhes – cell, sail, *Seil* (rope) –

        We pass on –

into a bright wide sparkle,
sun beating the very devil from the water
in jazzed up silver blue held taut
above the horizontal surface,
ducks' necks stretched up in rippled light,
the brimming edges fringed
with soft tall grass –

        We pass on –

what is this urging?
Do we prefer quick slits of time,
fear loss of pitch in slowing, stopping,
prefer to guard the wonder, promise
of the glimpses,
and wind our way
still taunted by the sun
into parched hills
where evening comes?

December in Aveyron

water at the weir's
steel lip
bronze flecked
from bracken
bridles at
the coming
endless tumble
moss flash
on stones and trunks
the catch of setting sun
on tawny plumage
as a kite lifts off

        chance angles
        from our spot

        they don't need us
        don't need our gaze

the track stays level
while birches bend
pipe cleaners
on slither slope
and through a mesh
of leafless trees
a massive shaft of rock
thrusts up
old as starlight
erect against the wash of time
the chiselling at its feet.

Prue Chamberlayne

Maisemore Weir

Bubbles trail swiftly,
in the silver centre
between ballooning withies,
the tar works chimney,
holds steady down the middle.
This smooth and solid slipping,
untroubled, unsuspecting,
turns the bend
and meets the drop –
hastens over,
white with tension,
banks up brown
against the counter-surge
that froths and pounds,
ruffled as far as the eye can see –
how long to soothe its troubles?

*

One winter my father
came here, meadows crisp and hard,
river frozen, doubtless creaking,
and walked across,
thrilled at his daring,
to meet my mother with child,
mindful of dark depths
and sucking under.

Prue Chamberlayne started writing poetry following a career teaching and researching in comparative social policy and biographical methods. She grew up on a farm in Gloucestershire, travelled widely in Europe and Africa, and lives in London. A favourite place for writing is a deserted valley in the Aveyron in France.

Tim Cockburn

Deco
Sex and the City
Carrots in the ground tend not to make a virtue of withdrawnness
Variation on a microwave warning sticker
Reminder about the songs currently in the charts
To Chelsey in the Bentinck Hotel

Deco

I love you because you are like love
a flimsy and preposterous thing,
like a deco bedside cabinet
whose gold trim is coming away,
whose quilted sides are yellow and punctured,
but that you buy anyhow,
if only because, among the serious junk,
its cheerful stab at flair seems
a certain defiance, a retort.

Sex and the City

walking to a garage not because
you want anything but because
at home everyone is shoving into each other

staring at a carton of juice
which shows an orange skipping with a cane
and two grapes laughing at the orange

**Carrots in the ground tend not to make
a virtue of withdrawnness,**

so it's easier to snatch one from it
than it is a person, though that too is possible.

*

I'm not going to say it was withdrawnness
you snatched me from
– that would be too dramatic by far, though it's true
that by a hillock in September and later a bar
you got me pretty much over my 'summer's suspicion'
(that *although in company I may appear to be interested
and engaged, I am primarily concerned with protecting
and ultimately retreating to a private defensive inner-world
to which I deem human intimacy a threat*, etcetera).
    Pretty much over,
though perhaps I should have held on for dear life:
then would your victory have been the sweeter?

*

But it wasn't a victory, was it? Not for you.
I hate the idea of women recalling men from sulks
as some kind of sport, and is it sulking
just to feel a little *vertically displaced*?
Robert Frost has written of the poetic trance,
and yes, perhaps he's right, but few poets I've met
would like it ever to be thought that with their special compulsion
they present a special problem.
Frankly I'd like very much to seem
an 'immodestly accurate transcription of a dream'.

*

Tim Cockburn

Which utterly you were that Sunday
when we walked though some woods
and then back along the Fakenham Road
and we didn't hold hands though I think
we wanted to and slapping the pavement with a stick
I couldn't believe you were here
you were so lovely in your crumpled blue scarf
and love itself was a bowlful of water
we carried between us and every passer-by
we bade look and they looked
and saw in it a brilliant and terrible fish
and we said, *Yes, we're every bit as astonished
by it as you are, we can't even remember
who entrusted it to us in the first place.*

                *

It was getting on, and from across the field
you called to me, *Just one more*,
because always you knew there had to be
a bigger, madder one, hiding. (Didn't it draw in
even the finest of its fine hairs, and come gladly?)

Carrots in the ground tend not to make a virtue of withdrawnness

Variation on a microwave warning sticker

Check standing items frequently, and stir.
Leave nothing unattended (this is in case
delayed eruptive boiling should occur).

Take him: he loves you, yes? Within a year
or two he'll miss the danger, miss the chase.
He could do now. Check frequently, and stir.

Wear lovers through or drop as you prefer;
if you won't replace because you *can* replace
delayed eruptive boiling may occur.

Conviction, kindness – these things drain. (To where
so surely, so like colour from a face?)
They may return. Check frequently, or stir.

Life is flux, the manic screens infer,
invite it into yours, or in its place
delayed eruptive boiling will occur.

Better to wait on stubborn water, or
affect its leaping, when in either case
you could be burned (stress *could be*)? Waters, stir.
Delayed, eruptive: boiling must occur.

Tim Cockburn

Reminder about the songs currently in the charts

They mean how beautiful and near she is.
Though now each asks no more than to rest
an elbow on your consciousness
as a tired lane swimmer pauses for breath
at the end of the pool, then pushes away again,
when they do it won't be forever;
they will catch you in some bar or bedroom
and mean how beautiful and near she is.

To Chelsey in the Bentinck Hotel

Sometimes in going to pick something up,
however casually certain your fingers it is one thing,
looking may show it to be another,
just as sometimes in telling someone you love them,
however casually certain your tongue the words are true,
on the ear they may fall as forced or artificial,
and in saying them you may come to realise you don't,
or not as you thought, and it will seem
a kind of sneakiness on the part of the words,
as it does on the part of my lager, when playing pool
I swig from it and it is not my lager
but your lager top, or even in coming to write a poem,
when it shrugs at you from the page and says,
No poem here, only the bones of one at best,
and those you reject as too deliberate or too cute,
since always it is possible that for forty minutes
exactly my lager is a lager, on my ears on my tongue
to the touch I love you, and this is the Bentinck Hotel.

Tim Cockburn was born in Banbury, Oxfordshire, and grew up in Nottingham. In 2007 he completed a BA in Creative Writing at the Norwich School of Art and Design.

Bryan Heiser

Another Ithaca

For Oliver Bernard

Another Ithaca

1

'The Sirens' song' he says 'has poisoned my blood:
I took the wax from my ears as we sailed past
that island. All day I was like a God, stood
listening: me and the man tied to the mast …

Can one drown their singing in one's own song,
hold the darlings under till the bubbles stop,
and the lovely faces relax, who so long
has sailed secretly to where the notes drop

as nymphs and naiads on the sand before me,
when my hand moves without thought to my thighs,
so that I can't think beyond what I can see
inside my skull where the imagined honey lies?

I'll never be cured. Though sometimes a reprieve
fools me into thinking I am whole again,
then I hear music. I have learned not to believe:
redemption's for stupider or stronger men.

We are both marked: he will leave Penelope,
and I will never do all that I might do,
which is hubris once more, I know: but look me
in the eye and tell me that it isn't so.

Another drink.' he says. 'I have lost everything
men hold valuable. When they call I go
and so would you if you had heard the Sirens sing:
it's here, in your palm: take it from me. I know.'

2

'There's never surf in that enchanted water,
neither storm nor other men will ever reach
where the soft footfall of the lotus-porter
only briefly disturbs the still, dreaming beach

where vacancy pools thickly around the dreamer
and dreaming slowly unspools infinity
weightless as the smoke from the unseen steamer
that stains the unfathomable night sky.

But all this is noise. My voice offends my ears:
I've nothing useful to say; and these eyes see
nothing that oughtn't reduce a man to tears
when he might sleep comforted beside that sea.

Another drink. Enough brings forgetfulness
I would trade misery for that, sweet and clean,
if I knew how. And how forget the caress
of the beauty I have tasted, heard and seen?

That is what keeps me here when I could have slept
eternity away, but there is a truth,
a bargain I see you think easily kept:
wait till you have only memories of youth.'

3

'Last night? In a gutter in my own puke:
what's it to you? Do you imagine a drink
buys you rights? God, you look like you've seen a spook.
Go away. Can't a man have some room to think?

And don't imagine I looked up at the stars:
I was blind drunk, like the other pigs I keep
company with. And in winter behind bars
usually: if it gets too cold I can't sleep.

Here's my girl: cheap red wine. She shares my sty,
her and Poppy, a slut like her mother.
They stop me caring how far I've gone awry
and God I'm thankful for that. Get me another.

They'll kill me, and they can, any time they want
for all I care. Look here, would you want to live:
bleary eyes, foul breath and soiled underpants?
I'm waiting for the oblivion they'll give

Today, tomorrow, next day: what's it matter?
Won't be long till I give all this the heave-ho
and you'll sit here looking smug and getting fatter
and I won't give a shit because I won't know.'

4

'Mood swings? Me? Sod off! No, I apologise:
come back and have a drink. You're probably right.
It's the wine and a head full of seagull cries;
I'm three sheets to the wind and not thinking straight.

"Steer middle course, right?" the smart bastard tells me,
"That's the trick." But he can't tell me how to smell
which wind it is blows that way, nor what the sea
might have in store for us over the next swell.

Scylla and Charybdis: and seagulls mewing
while ankle deep in blood and shipmates' entrails
those of us still able to, stand up hewing
clawed or scaled or feathered hands from the taffrails

and braver men than me screaming for mothers
as they disappear down into great foetid
maws and the hungry seagulls' blood-red feathers,
and the things we had to do, and things I did.

But long hours between the naiads' salty thighs,
slippery with loving: I promise you, lad,
that's not something you forget; and Gods! their cries –
hearing them is enough to make a man mad.'

5

'Buy me a bottle to say goodbye,' he says.
'A last good bottle before I up and go:
I greet each new place with such fine promises
and my promises last no longer than snow.

Familiarity breeds what they say:
I can only take so much – and I see you
can hardly wait for me to be on my way.
So. I'm going to find somewhere that's clean and new,

except there's no such place, somewhere that I'll find
a woman. And I could get work: I can graft
hard as the next derelict if I set my mind.
Don't look at me like I've gone fucking daft.

I need a woman – if any will have me –
long as when we've both finished, then I can sleep
and through her body feel the green heaving sea,
and hear the promises the sirens keep.'

He stared at me for a long moment blankly,
then blinked and got unsteadily to his feet,
and picking up the wine bottle walked away
without a backward look out into the street.

Bryan Heiser has been writing poetry for decades: in London where he worked in local and regional government, and now in rural Norfolk where he lives with his wife. His work has been published in *Home* by *Katabasis*, *Murray Street* by *The Poetry School* (after Bryan's home where the long poem workshop met for two years) and other publications.

Mary Laxton

The Carpet Bag
A lesson from the Cepizun moon
The Rain Turtle
The Flea
Towards an act of heroism
Wishful

The Carpet Bag

Slightly awkward as if place lost:
old mother's spur-winged womb.

Its handles cling on to what's gone,
when sack was nearly new;
plumped with lining, ferrous red,
perfect enough to hold water,
and weight –

and in that expectant space,
a glorious usefulness swelled
for its purse of perfect sample;

from parts laid out on a table,

    cut from the pattern of a secret.

A lesson from the Cepizun* moon

I glimpsed a gate-hurdling wolf
on the path to the hills. I dared to look
and suddenly, I became the ground she fixed on –
pinned down
by piercing ice-blue cross-eyed peculiarity.
And I let her in –
so that she could breathe her history to claim me for her own.

She told me
I was the green hide hunted,
to be defleshed
and soaked in water,
so that everything I was,
would be rubbed together and smoked before eagle month had come.
Going-up-hill-of-things nodded and fell back to gather dye-plants for the climb,
while I was pegged and stretched,
in sunlight and in moonlight,
mumbling to a sky of air as dryness worked my leather.

And now,
I am tanned,
and see you wolf for who you are,

>and I will walk this old month's path barefoot from now on,
>and barefoot, I will dance in the month of little frog, the month
>the leaves come out, the month the birds fly south –
>and the people on the hills might teach me many other ways,
>and help me skin and tan the likes of even you,

although you need to know one thing:
that you will be nothing unless I so choose.

And yet, you teach me.

*name given to a February moon by the Cree

The Rain Turtle

stick meet sand
wester out to neb-mound
ovolo down
gnomon-yoked to soft ground

oviposit next
whittle shell with doily trim
table set with matted crest
rivet plate to nature's grid
add the limbs
but keep her graphics plain
lens-curve strong
ridged to fubsy nub

and rain

Look up and see
the cloudage come.
Was that sound the turtle drum?
Javelin-man?

From that first lump of mud,
grandmother has borne the weight,
so gratitude is not to pierce her side,
with stick that is, just so, a stick
which cannot kill or feed a hunter's pride.

Come, it will, the rain
from she who sings it.

Come, it will.

Mary Laxton

The Flea

I don't want to sleep with you because of that flea.
It came off the dog and I didn't want a dog
but you insisted, so it was your job
to treat the thing and because you didn't, there are fleas everywhere.
Thirty eggs a day. That's what you need to address,
not my eggs. I have only one or two anyway,
and it's not the right time so there's little point,
although I know you don't think of eggs at all,
but I do, because I want a baby, not sex.
Ouch! See, it bit me!
And don't give me that both-our-blood-is-mingled-because-it-has-bitten-you-too story.
You can only use that once and it was done. Long ago.
I acquiesced, remember? It was very clever, using a third party:
made me look elsewhere, share the logic,
feel close to you by thinking the same thing about a thing.
And you did have a point about the murder weapon
being only a fingernail but it doesn't work anymore.
Your conceit is mine now and I'm quite happy to murder that flea
and murder you for not treating the dog.
There'll be blood on the sheets before the night is out,
and that's another reason ...

Towards an act of heroism

Yes, this will do: this poem's face sits in
My mirror's frame; serves as my reflection
When I want it to. So who am I?
I could describe the dimples in my cheeks
Except I only have them when I smile.
I could explain the dark rings round my eyes
But then I'd have to lie and let out more
Untruths to cover up what's going on
And let myself be seen by the very
Person I don't really wish to involve
In all of this. Instead, I'll brush my hair
And let my mirror's image do the work.

Wishful

As long as

the left eye remains,
      it will be all right,
moon will be moon not the thing that lights the night
and it will declare ignorance, round and willing
like a favourite chubby pottery mug bobbing jolly in old water.
So,   moon   (right eye winks)
I need your timely crescent
to scythe through things that aren't;
scrape down all to my buried bones (no bones, no bones)
and if they're gone when all is gone,
when there's nothing left
                      .
           except that eye

Mary Laxton was born in Llangollen in Wales in 1964 and studied English Literature and Language at the University of Birmingham. She has worked in the television industry and as a secondary school teacher. She now lives in Norfolk with her husband and three children.

David Lebor

The Size of Winter
The double life of pigeons
Aufgesetzt auf den Bergen des Herzens
Cuenca – Madrid
Squatters

The Size of Winter

          The sky discloses
an iron claw the size of winter;
blackbirds scatter back
from glowing apples.

Where trees with great wrists stretch back
under their own weight,
blackbirds nodded and shook their beaks
like lamplighters looking for wicks.

The dark holes in the hedge
are blackbirds.

The double life of pigeons

Flight startles you free
of your paranoid nodding. You trip

into a synchrony that a little boy directs
with imagined kite strings.

The earth wants to keep you,
tugging your hulls at the completion
of each wing beat – oars
against the undertow.
I watch you break off

within an outlying arc,
drawn only in retrospect
by your return, as when a flute wanders
and rejoins the melody.

You pulled a cargo of sky between you, tipped it
so close to the balcony, air thumped
through the room.
My thoughtspeed caught up with your pulse,
identifying the quills
of your hubbub wingbeat,

when the sun lit a beacon,
you pocketed your wings
and shambled back to chivvy
a musket of old men in waistcoats.

Aufgesetzt auf den Bergen des Herzens

(Exposed on the mountains of the heart) Rilke

{an encounter with a Russian in Austria}

*Warum schreibst? Ich weiss es
besser, als du es weisst.*
– I met the Moscow heir,
who reserved the mountain for a day
to face the snow alone –
*My wife left. Her child,
her daughter, died skiing
in Finland, 1991.
Do you think of character as visible?
I couldn't see myself
in the mirror, only recognise.
I couldn't see past my sight,
past my eyes.*

The chair-lifts with their English posture,
slung from a hook, transported us
over elbows of rock.

I know the life of the poor ...
His father solved a shortage
of phone numbers.
*(That was the dial to his safe.)
... they take winter to heart
if they can't heat their homes;
would rather hang
than stay with the wrong neighbour.
What's that Goethe about Gods, after
'Sie schreiten vom Berge
Zu Bergen hinueber?' ...*

David Lebor

'The men they lift up
Must fear them doubly.'
The one thing we can't see
is ourselves.

He'd scolded her daughter once
for leaving with wet hair.
She returned in an outrage of winter midges,
the burn of graupel on her face.
I know why you write
more than you. My uncle, a writer,
couldn't catch sight
of his words.
Look at me. _____. Bitte!
You can see
what I cannot. Find me
behind these useless eyes.

Tell me why I am here.

Cuenca – Madrid

(Journey returning from a wedding)

    i

Castile-La Mancha is chock-full of iron:
matchsticks of abandoned rail,
the carcasses of chemical plants,
riverbeds of grit
like stitches on leather;
rusty lichen. Its people,
its black trees, scarce and willing.

    ii

The train slows,
inches by *Calle Carril del Puente*,
a yard from somebody's back room:
the frame of a face from a picture
looking out at a travelling film.

    iii

Tarrançon ~ a town of cold chalk,
car queues, of schoolchildren
taking the side-streets home.

A crop twists up
out of red soil
like cloves out of an orange.
And, for the first time, birds:
magpies,
wearing black and white as colour.

David Lebor

iv

A man sits, and rests his eyelids.
Skin hangs over disappearing lips, out
over his neck. His knuckles interlock;
I find that mine are interlocked.
The train tosses his head out of sleep.

v

After *Aranjuez*, an express station
with immaculate clocks, he speaks to me –
I betrayed certain thoughts.
The first winter he left for Madrid,
he had asked about the flocks
migrating alongside the train.
A sign, his father had said,
a salutation from the city.

vi

The Cuenca wedding guests
have scattered into Spain.

Images of life
                beyond the carriage window;
vertigo at the thought
of unknown lives.
                Something is punctured.

Pallets, warehouse hamlets,
a history in trackside litter,
the sucker punch of passing freight …

*

I am not ready for marriage.

A journey:
the door slams. We commit
to a world behind Plexiglas, to a view
of the procession.
I wish myself out among it.

Squatters

Do not let them past your locks!
They are casting off their clothes,
recalibrating statutes,
inviting you to own them.
Smell a rat
and the nest comes alive.
They guard the dwelling in shifts
with a solicitor's nous. You had the access
boarded up, but one wet November ...
and the wood rot
came apart in their hands.

This is a fault line:

in their eyes they are a parliament
of owls, their tenure primeval.
Even the law
answers to instinct. So where
were the rodents when I accepted their food?
The girl had a charm. She offered me
her kaleidoscope, as you might offer
a folder of consonants to enlighten a tourist.
I tried to sit upright, to cross my knees.
I wanted to ask her, who will clean the drains?
But the walls were sidling further.
Last month this was a building.

David Lebor grew up in Kent. He was poet of the 50th anniversary Spoleto Festival. His poems have been read on *NPR* and *RTE 1*. He was runner-up in the National Poetry Competition BT prize, and has exhibited poems in San Francisco with paintings by Nicholas Halligan. He studied French and German at Oxford.

Katherine Venn

Three Children
Plough Monday
Writing
The Guest

Three Children

1.

They were staying at her grandparents' house, a foreign
place of creaks and loudly ticking clocks;
heavy furniture, dark wood, a yew-filled garden

to explore. Best of all, a trip to the toyshop
where they could each – unknown delight – choose anything
they wanted. It was so beautiful it stopped

her where she stood. She knew she had to bring
it home with her. It looked so small and helpless,
its wide blue eyes delicately fringed

with eyelashes. With proper seriousness
she mothered it; found a shoebox bed;
decided she would bathe it; arranged its dress.

But later when she went to pat its head
and touch those gorgeous lashes, they came away
on her finger. All of them. *The water*, she said,

as her heart lurched and tried to work out the shape
of the awful thing she'd done. *Spoilt her brand-new
gift. Hurt her baby. So she scraped*

the accusing lashes up and threw
them down behind her bed. But a thought kept
prodding her, too sad to sleep that night: she knew

she'd made things even worse. *If only I'd let
him know, Daddy could have fixed her.* The stark
fact tormented her. Too late; and so she wept,

the lashes like spiders under the bed, in the dark.

2.

He liked to sit in his mother's sewing-room –
more of a cupboard, really, cluttered with all
her little bits of kit. In the gloom

of autumn evenings he'd lean against the wall
and watch her as she worked, or shut his eyes and listen
to the *snick* of heavy scissors through cloth, the fall

and rise of the sewing-machine that gathered and lessened
as her foot pressed the pedal on the floor –
falling quiet as she stopped to adjust the tension,

squint to thread a needle, or swing open the little door
at the machine's base to wind the bobbin. He'd pad
around the room, poking through boxes and drawers:

the stars of pins in their black velvet cushion, the sad
smell of plastic measuring tapes, the felt
wallet of wicked needles. What made him glad

were the neat ranks of cotton reels. He knelt
to touch their little pegs, move them along
like beads on an abacus; counted and felt

the different colours. Just one thing didn't belong:
their labels. They spoilt the pleasing order, were messy –
scrappy bits of paper that looked all wrong,

begging to be peeled off. So, in a kind of ecstasy,
one day he did – relishing the work he'd begun,
the thought of his mother smiling at his sweet conspiracy,

at what he had so kindly, neatly, done.

3.

Her Granny made it for her: a rag doll
in a pretty flowered dress, with lemon-yellow
wool for hair, in bunches. *Emily*, she called,

and picked it up to look, to touch. *Hello*,
she said, fingering the sewn-shut eyes, each
lash a length of thread, stitched into the pillow

of its soft, wide face, which was much too big;
but never mind. It might look slightly strange
but she'd been taught that beauty often hid

in unlikely places. Things quickly changed
when she saw it couldn't sit up straight,
with the other toys, all neatly arranged

for a tea party. Its neck bent under the weight
of the too-large head, and softly flopped
onto its chest, as though it couldn't stay awake.

Come on, she said, and reached across to prop
it up. *Wake up*. Its head lolled forward.
Please, through gritted teeth. Again it dropped.

Enraged, she scooped it up and flung it in a cupboard.
Stupid doll, she said. *You're no fun*.
But for months after she was troubled,

as though it were a friend she'd shunned.
And so she ran to rescue it, with its calm
and docile face, in tears for what she'd done;

the doll's head sagging heavy in her arms.

Plough Monday

and celebration's set aside again,
gives way to steady, head-down stamp and sigh
of turning up the earth, the year's field
curving to meet a blank sky.

The broken soil is heavy on your feet.
But remember as you walk the loam:
you're hitched to an older beast, who knows. Yield
to his pace as he pulls – home.

Writing

mid-October, towards the year's winding down
and the morning's cracked wide open

the rain that's just passed slicks the asphalt paths
that line the park
and lend it sudden flare and shine

you run its margins slowly

and loop around the trees in a kind of cursive
your route dutiful repetitions of the letter 'o'

(leaves like paper cut-outs
are bullied by a wind that would make something of them)

a clumsy body grasped by the mind
and pushed along, unwilling,
dragging as though against the earth's grain

– a falling forward into words

thoughts flap off like seagulls from wet grass
as all narrows to this
just one step
after another

The Guest

You made yourself at home inside my head
and now there's only room for thoughts of you.
My days lie ruined, like an unmade bed –

I wish we shared one. Smiling, you quietly spread
your words out for me, watched them as they grew.
And made yourself at home inside my head.

Your image overlays each thought I tread,
a clouded pane of glass I strain to see through.
My days lie ruined like an unmade bed.

And now my own heart's writing goes unread:
I am a stranger to myself, preferring you,
since you made yourself at home inside my head.

We keep ourselves a secret, and instead
undress each other's words. Which must make do.
My days lie ruined, like an unmade bed.

And words don't count, don't last, is what you said.
Like these; but they're the only way I'll have you.
You made yourself at home inside my head.
My days lie ruined, like an unmade bed.

Katherine Venn fell in love with poetry as a child when she was read Walter de la Mare's 'The Listeners'; she fell in love with contemporary poetry when she read Alice Oswald's *Dart*. Born in South London, she read English at Oxford and spent her twenties working in publishing.

Julia Webb

Full Circle
Lent
After cleaning out your house
Feather Factory
After
Thetford Forest

Full Circle

You anti-Jesused me in two-two-time
flying down the hoop of your guitar-pick backbone,
squeeze-boxed and gramophoned
in smoggy small town backrooms
where we scrolled and scrolled.

Later bus-busted on dirty milk crates
rubbing along in a tatty red transit
with the hulked beasts of Marshall amps,
beer sticky drums and hard-nosed flight cases
your arms caught me as we lurched round every bend.

Next you found me in the slow running away
of party nights: shag-piled bathrooms, spiral steps
leading down to the muddiness of the river bank
and you with your own push and shove agenda,
and ears deaf to no.

Later still in smoky wine-barred eighties
you announced regret as a kiss off the old block:
snatched me into a new year's embrace, catapulted us back
to the moment when you lent down from the stage,
offered me your wristband – and I put it on.

Lent

We talked about the pitfalls of summer babies, those BAD-UNS gone to seed and Whitsun weddings, Easter when it falls early and the time we found all that CHOCOLATE that she had GIVEN UP for Lent hidden in the bottom of the cleaning closet. And how we despised the way she cried and said *Please* DON'T *tell your Daddy* – as if we would! But we liked to imagine his big bitumen hands resting on the faded skin of the BIBLE and his stern and serious face and the: *Mary you know you have done WRONG!* But Alice she took all that chocolate and we ate it up in the yard burying the silver foil deep beneath the compost heap where only JESUS could see it. Alice says JESUS can see everything – he can even see through walls. Sometimes I think about that when I'm in the bathroom and I pull the raspy towel close over me but it's hard to wash that way – and even harder when Mamma is shouting: *Come downstairs at once and go and get some potatoes* and Alice is whispering through the door: *Hurry up in there, Mikey will be here soon and I need to get ready.* And then I remember how she KISSED Mikey in the car and I wonder why she isn't worried about JESUS seeing THAT and about the whole threat of MORTAL SIN? Mamma says that autumn births are the WORST because you have to go all through the long hot summer and Daddy puts his hand on the holy book and says: *We won't talk of SUCH THINGS.* And then I remember the chocolate in the closet and how good it tasted and I am about to say something because I don't want to go to HELL, but Alice kicks me hard in the shin and I see Mamma shaking her head with her long shine of hair and I remember the sharp sting of Daddy's hand. So when he looks at me with his caterpillar eyebrows raised THAT WAY I just lower my head and say NOTHING and know that presently we will eat dinner which will be ham and peas and POTATOES and I concentrate hard on my plate and imagine that I am JESUS and that I am eating up all the world's SIN.

Julia Webb

After cleaning out your house

I wanted to rush home and throw everything away,
cram the details into bin bags
and toss them onto the back seat of the car.
I wanted to mix letters
with plates and underwear,
sweep them (like a bonfire waiting for the match)
into the middle of the floor,
or shovel them out of the open mouths
of the windows and doors.
I wanted to open up the house wide
invite the wind and the trees inside.
I wanted to throw away the windows,
the doors, the front path, the weeds,
the cars, the people walking along the street,
turn the kitchen cupboards inside out,
uncook all those breakfasts and dinners,
turn on the taps until the water ran dry.

Feather Factory

We kiss by the side of the feather factory,
the stench of singed wings
fills our noses and mouths.

We are nest-bound – tongues entwined,
pockets full of Swan Vestas and Players Number Six,
your nylon trousers spark to the rub.

Later the birds will haunt us:
their feathers will float around our heads,
pillow our eyes against the brightness of the day.

Julia Webb

After

It's like unreeling
yards and yards of tangled wire,
or finding mice in an attic
you never even knew you had.
It's like the wash-off, run-through,
bleed-right hours of sorting.

It's like squirrelling backwards,
or finding yourself back in the town
that you spent years getting out of.
It's like a thousand keys without a lock,
(or a thousand locks without a key).

It's the unravelled jumper syndrome
of clutter-mouth, skip-face, charity-bone.
It's those sweets in a bowl that your Nana saved.
It's the pencilled words in the book
that you gave your mother and she defaced.

We hunt in ghost-corners,
suck dust balls, brave snowstorms, spiders,
slave away for garage-vanned days
and mop-floored hours,
traverse the piles in drawers and cupboards.

It's like a shoe-shine crystal avalanche,
an amalgamation of days and nights and nights and days.
It's hair on a brush and teeth in a bag.
It's a dirty bathroom and unwashed plates.

Thetford Forest

Frozen mud-pelt of the early morning.
The air bristles with frost-shine,

our winter breath hangs
whitening momentarily in the air before us.

On into deep grey dark,
where the trees close in on us,

a gentle crackle in the glooming,
rolling pine cones and rabbit droppings,

faraway bird-call and the startle-flap
of a fresh waked pigeon.

Deer-eye startles, twigs fire rounds
of snapper-jawed ammunition,

spiky fingers gnarl,
chipper of wood-peel, crack and splinter.

Finally we are out amongst
left over leaf-mould

into the stark-limbed skeleton
of the deciduous forest.

The sky opens out – a gap of relief
after the ink-smudge conifers.

We gulp lung after lung of early winter,
see every third tree marked with a cross,

a yellow smear
where the saw will bite,

flaking jackets of bark barely
covering pale bodies,

blood-sap stinks up the air
with its honey-thick sweetness.

Julia Webb grew up in Thetford. She has a degree in Creative Writing from Norwich University College of the Arts. Her work has been published in *Ink, Sweat and Tears*, *Veto*, and *Spring* (Gatehouse Press). In 2009 she was runner-up for Café Writers Norfolk Commission. She currently lives in Norwich.

Sam Wright

Constellation
Summer heat
Beachcombing
The day Orion fired his arrow
Birdsong
Three wishes

This is Homer's soil that we are walking upon
Solomos

Constellation

We step to the car
the garden pricked with lines
of moonlight
of rainfall

we talk of
what happened
what could happen
what should happen

Yet sometimes
    in among these happenings

we forget to glance upward
and see Orion's bow
stretched like a tendon

and be reminded
that the gods still stand

pinned to the sky

hearing every footstep,
          every crunch of gravel

Summer heat

The light may have been drugged;
vague and sluggish,
part of a world
that's been sent to rest,

but watch carefully
and there is still movement –

someone drops
a half-eaten apple, another
sneezes wetly
into the palm of his hand.

Over the road, a dog arches its piss
against the dry skin of the tarmac.

And in the middle of it all
a shape stumbles
through the street,

not animal or human,
or anything in between,

but still looking hopefully
for a window to open.

I want to own this place.
I want it to be mine
like the lint in my pockets.

Beachcombing

Among the sand,
each piece looks like bone,
ribs and vertebrae
cracked and scattered,
femur and fibula ground into salt.

Today, my dream
is to bring it back to life,
to gather each pale scrap
and calmly lay it out in line,

to dust it clean with my fingers
as I form ligaments from kelp beds,
pressing driftwood patiently
down into marrow.

Then, and only then,
I will ask the sea
to wash the death
from the shore,

listening carefully
to the wet gurgle of silt
sinking into muscle,

the gentle lapping
of water on rock,

the smoothing of everything
back into sand.

The day Orion fired his arrow

First came the dull whine,
as if the universe had fallen

down an octave,
purring like a struck bell
muffled in cloth.

Next, a hiss of moving air
as apples began to topple
from the trees.

Later, someone would claim
that the insects turned

suddenly in the air,
scared from their paths

by a silhouette something
like a bird of prey.

But then, silently, came the light,
as if the sun had chosen

to rise in the north, south,
east and west at once,

the world's curve lit
from every angle.

Time hung like this, shadowless,
and seconds passed into minutes

until the hot glow forced
each and every eye to lower.

And then, as sudden as a bomb
or the crack of a rifle,

it was dark again, and countless
necks strained towards the sky;

confused, exhausted, and waiting
for a second shot.

Birdsong

Someone once told me
that one day,
quite by accident,

the birds will all
strike a chord
bright and clean enough

to draw the sweat
from the surface of the Earth.

I'm not sure that this is true.

But if I am wrong,
then let me be first
among the water

as it rises, kneading
the salt left underfoot
with my toes

as if it were a blanket
of crushed diamonds.

Sam Wright

Three wishes

My first is to draw the colour from the skies
   until they hang empty,
   a screen purged of its image,
   no flicker to distract itself.

My second is for the seas to calm,
   the waves' breath slowing
   as it settles into agar,
   a cool, blank glow
   held firm in its surface.

Then, when the world is just horizon,
   my third will be for all light
   to bring itself to rest,
   the darkness gnawing its way through
   to exhaustion.

Tomorrow, I will have three more wishes;
   to watch the sky bruise with colour,
   the seas whisper back to life,

and, last of all, to listen peacefully
   as you begin to wake.

Sam Wright graduated with a BA in Creative Writing from Norwich University College of the Arts (NUCA) in 2007. Sam has since worked as a freelance writer, journalist and web developer. He lives in Norwich with his wife, Anna.